SPOTLIGHT ON CIVIC ACTION

COMMUNITY SERVICE AND VOLUNTEERING

MARCO ANDRES

PowerKiDS press.

NEW YORK

Published in 2018 by The Rosen Publishing Group, Inc.
29 East 21st Street, New York, NY 10010

Editor: Melissa Raé Shofner
Book Design: Michael Flynn
Interior Layout: Reann Nye

Photo Credits: Cover, p. 13 Hero Images/Getty Images; p. 4 George Silk/The LIFE Images Collection/Getty Images; p. 5 marino bocelli/Shutterstock.com; p. 6 barbsimages/Shutterstock.com; p. 7 (background) Evgeny Karandaev/Shutterstock.com; p. 7 (photograph) Courtesy of the Library of Congress; pp. 8, 26 wavebreakmedia/Shutterstock.com; pp. 9, 29 Monkey Business Images/Shutterstock.com; p. 11 Sergey Nivens/Shutterstock.com; p. 15 https://commons.wikimedia.org/wiki/File:US_Navy_090806-N-6220J-004_Sailors_and_Navy_Delayed_Entry_Program_members_serve_breakfast_to_homeless_men; p. 16 szefei/Shutterstock.com; p. 17 India Picture/Shutterstock.com; p. 18 Tui De Roy/Minden Pictures/Getty Images; p. 19 Mila Supinskaya Glashchenko/Shutterstock.com; p. 20 ESB Professional/Shutterstock.com; p. 21 Rawpixel.com/Shutterstock.com; p. 23 asiseeit/E+/Getty Images; p. 25 Blend Images - KidStock/Brand X Pictures/Getty Images; p. 27 Dragon Images/Shutterstock.com; p. 28 mangostock/Shutterstock.com.

Cataloging-in-Publication Data

Names: Andres, Marco.
Title: Community service and volunteering / Marco Andres.
Description: New York : PowerKids Press, 2018. | Series: Spotlight on civic action | Includes index.
Identifiers: ISBN 9781538327906 (pbk.) | ISBN 9781508164029 (library bound) | ISBN 9781538328026 (6 pack)
Subjects: LCSH: Voluntarism--United States--Juvenile literature. | Voluntarism--Juvenile literature. | Teenage volunteers in social service--United States--Juvenile literature.
Classification: LCC HN90.V64 A53 2018 | DDC 302′.14--dc23

Manufactured in the United States of America

CPSIA Compliance Information: Batch #BW18PK For further information contact Rosen Publishing, New York, New York at 1-800-237-9932.

CONTENTS

CHAPTER ONE

MAKING A DIFFERENCE

Community service is work that's done without pay. It's a form of civic engagement, which is the act of people coming together to **enact** change that benefits their community. A community may be a group of people who live or work in the same place or a group of individuals with common interests, values, or goals. An individual often belongs to several communities, so there are many opportunities to make a difference.

On January 20, 1961, President John F. Kennedy addressed the nation and said, "Ask not what your country can do for you—ask what you can do for your country."

Community service is sometimes required by an individual's school or workplace. Volunteering is when you do nonrequired community service on your own time simply because you want to make a difference.

If you've ever picked up trash in a park or helped at a bake sale, you've done community service. These are just a few types of community service, though—there are many ways for you to get involved! Helping out and making a difference in your community can be fun and rewarding.

CHAPTER TWO

BENEFITS FOR EVERYONE

Community service and volunteer work are great ways to give back and make a difference in your community. By giving your time, sharing your services, or **donating** needed items, you can enact positive change and improve the lives of others. What you may not realize, though, is that you'll benefit, too.

Community service and volunteering give individuals a chance to explore their interests and meet new people. Volunteers also gain valuable experience and learn about new points of view. When you volunteer in your community, you'll likely learn a lot about yourself and the world. You may also make new friends and have a lot of fun.

The cycle of giving to a community and receiving benefits in return may be described as a **reciprocal** relationship. There are benefits for everyone involved.

GIRL SCOUTS AT THE WHITE HOUSE, 1916

Juliette Gordon Low founded the Girl Scouts of America in 1912. For more than 100 years, young Girl Scouts across the country have been **empowered** by their experiences in volunteer work.

CHAPTER THREE

ARE YOU READY?

Community service and volunteer work are great ways to become more involved in your community. Before getting involved with a service project, there are a few important questions you should ask yourself. Volunteering can be a serious commitment, and it's easier to stay **motivated** if you enjoy and believe in what you're doing.

Do you prefer to work alone or with other people? Would you rather work directly with those in need or help an organization with office duties? Answering these questions will help you decide where and how to volunteer.

Think about what makes you excited. Do you enjoy helping children? Do you enjoy working outside? You should also think about what you don't enjoy. It's probably not a good idea to volunteer at an animal shelter if you're allergic to cats and dogs. Also consider your strengths and skills. Do they fit with the project you're thinking about joining? Answer these questions honestly and it'll be easy to find volunteer work that matches your values and interests.

CHAPTER FOUR

TAKING THE TIME TO HELP

When considering community service or volunteering, you should think carefully about how much time you truly have to commit to a project. Many volunteer opportunities require a certain number of hours each week or month. This may not seem like a lot, but it can add up—especially when you may also need to attend school, finish your chores and homework, and play on a sports team. You might even have a part-time job.

Community service and volunteer projects don't pay, but you should still treat them like a job. When you sign up for a project, you're making a promise to help and people are depending on you to show up to do so. Be honest about how much time you can commit, and don't take on more than you can handle.

Some volunteer opportunities offer **flexible** hours. Whatever hours you choose, it's important to stick to them. Be reliable and show up on time.

CHAPTER FIVE

FINDING VOLUNTEER OPPORTUNITIES

Once you've thought about your interests and values and figured out how much time you can commit to a project, it's time to start looking for a place to volunteer. Talking to people is a great way to learn about opportunities in your community. For example, your teacher may know of another student who needs a **tutor** in a subject you're good at. Your mom or dad might know an elderly person in your neighborhood who could use help in their garden.

Your local library is another great place to look for community service and volunteer projects. A librarian may be able to tell you about local and national organizations that are looking for volunteers. You can also have an adult help you search online for community service and volunteer opportunities near where you live.

Libraries, churches, and community centers often have notice boards where people post messages for members of the community to see. Check these boards for opportunities to volunteer your time and services and give back to your community.

CHAPTER SIX

HELPING THOSE IN NEED

Community service and volunteering are about making life better for everyone. This may often involve helping people who are less fortunate. Check with homeless shelters in your area to see if there are any ways in which you can volunteer. Homeless shelters often need items such as toothpaste, soap, and blankets. They may also accept socks, shoes, and old reading glasses.

Many communities have a soup kitchen or food pantry. These are places that provide food for people in need. You may be able to help serve meals or **distribute** food. Another way to help is to donate nonperishable food items. If something is nonperishable, it won't easily spoil and can be stored for a long period of time. Canned and jarred foods are often nonperishable.

In 2009, members of the U.S. Navy served breakfast to the homeless at Dorothy's Soup Kitchen in Salinas, California. This was their way of giving back to the community during the Salinas Navy Week community service event.

CHAPTER SEVEN

PEOPLE OF ALL AGES

Many volunteer opportunities allow you to help other people directly. You may be able to tutor a younger student in math or help them learn to read. You could also volunteer with a youth sports team. Organizations such as Big Brothers Big Sisters pair children with older **mentors**. These programs give children an older friend to talk to and spend time with, which helps them reach their full **potential**.

There's a lot elderly people and young people can learn from each other. This is a great example of how reciprocal relationships work.

You might also enjoy helping an elderly person in your community. There may be someone in your neighborhood who needs help with daily chores. You could also volunteer at a nursing home. It's easy and fun to brighten an elderly person's day by taking time to play a board game, make a craft project, or simply talk with them.

CHAPTER EIGHT

ANIMALS IN NEED

Animals in your community may also be in need. Check with your local animal shelter to see if there are any volunteer opportunities available. Organizations such as the Society for the Prevention of Cruelty to Animals (SPCA) and other local animal shelters are often in need of volunteers. If you're old enough, you may be tasked with walking dogs, playing with kittens, feeding the shelter animals, or cleaning their cages.

Whales sometimes become beached, or stuck on the shore. Volunteers in New Zealand help keep a pilot whale and its calf wet while waiting for high tide to return.

If you love animals, volunteering at a local animal shelter is the perfect way for you to make a difference in your community. It's also a great way to gain valuable experience if you think you might want to work with animals when you're older.

Another interesting and fun way to volunteer with animals is to find a program in which children read to dogs in animal shelters. These types of programs help kids practice their reading skills in a judgement-free zone. It also gives the shelter dogs some much-needed attention and helps them build social skills. This increases their chances of being adopted.

CHAPTER NINE

SAVING THE PLANET

Earth is in need of some help these days, too. Luckily, there are many ways for you to improve and protect the **environment**. You might start by seeing if your school offers any community service or volunteer opportunities to plant trees, clean up trash, or collect cans and bottles for recycling.

Friends of the Earth International (FoEI) is an organization that works toward finding solutions for

Your town or city may organize community service projects for Arbor Day or Earth Day. Sign up and participate to make a difference in your community, but remember that every day is a good day to volunteer.

Earth's major environmental and social issues. Find which of its 75 national member groups is closest to you and see if you'd make a good volunteer.

You can also volunteer to help save **endangered** animals and their habitats through organizations such as the Wildlife Conservation Network. A habitat is the natural home of an animal, plant, or other living thing. As communities grow, construction and pollution may harm the surrounding environment.

CHAPTER TEN

TAKING POLITICAL ACTION

If you're interested in volunteering with a political **campaign**, you'll have to wait until you're in high school or college. After learning about the candidates running for office, you can choose to support whomever you'd like. Think about your values and those of the candidates. Who best represents your views and beliefs?

Once you've chosen someone to support, you can sign up to volunteer with their campaign. As a volunteer, you may have to make phone calls to potential voters on behalf of your chosen candidate. You may also hand out flyers or go door to door to speak with people in your community about a candidate. These activities are called canvassing. Canvassing helps identify supporters and share information about a candidate's campaign. As a canvasser, you may persuade an unsure voter to vote for your candidate.

As a volunteer, you may also be in charge of registering new voters. Volunteering with a campaign is a great way to learn about how politics work.

CHAPTER ELEVEN

SERVICE LEARNING

Some high schools and many colleges offer service-learning opportunities. Service learning combines community service work and educational instruction. At some schools, service learning is a requirement for graduation.

Service-learning opportunities may occur over holiday breaks or summer vacation. They may involve traveling to another state or sometimes another country, and you may need to pay for your travel costs. Service-learning trips may also require students to have special skills, such as knowing a foreign language.

On service-learning trips, students travel to places where they can make a difference, such as helping to rebuild homes after a hurricane or building a new school for a less fortunate community. Sometimes schools partner with outside organizations such as the National Youth Leadership Council or International Service Learning.

Habitat for Humanity is an organization that offers service-learning opportunities. You can volunteer to help build affordable homes for people in need during a break from school.

CHAPTER TWELVE

OTHER WAYS TO HELP

Not all community service and volunteering opportunities need to take place through an organization. There are many informal ways you can make a difference in your community all on your own. If you're often busy, creating your own community service project may be a good option for you. This will allow you to help others in need on your own time and at your own pace. Your project

Making greeting cards is a fun and creative community service project that will brighten someone else's day. You can send cards to people in the military or people in hospitals or nursing homes.

can be something you do on your own, or you can get your friends and family involved.

Your personal project may be a one-time activity, such as cleaning out your closet and donating your old clothes and toys to charity. It may also be something you do more often, such as a holding a food drive around Thanksgiving each year.

CHAPTER THIRTEEN

THINGS TO CONSIDER

Collecting items for donation is a great way to help charitable organizations. However, before organizing a food or clothing drive, you should contact the organization you hope to work with to ask what items it needs and wants. Sometimes an organization may have too much of one type of item and a strong need for something else. For example, an organization may receive a large number of baby toys

Some organizations have a greater need for certain items because of where they're located and who they're helping. Some organizations are in need of volunteers more than anything else.

around the holidays but have a strong need for toys for older children. Sometimes an organization may be in need of monetary donations more than anything else.

When contacting an organization about its needs or when dropping off a donation, you should also ask if volunteers are needed for anything else. An organization may need additional help sorting and distributing donated items.

CHAPTER FOURTEEN

GET STARTED TODAY

Community service and volunteering are necessary for the well-being of a community. By volunteering or participating in a community service project, you make a difference in the lives of those around you. This can be a very rewarding experience. You may even have fun and make some new friends.

If you're thinking about volunteering or creating your own community service project, you should consider the areas of need in your community. Also think about what you're interested in and what you care about. Where your values and the needs of your community overlap is the perfect place to begin your community service work.

If you want to help others, there are many ways you can start right now. Through volunteering and community service, you'll soon realize that even one person can make a big difference.

GLOSSARY

campaign (kam-PAYN) A plan to get a certain result, such as to win an election.

distribute (dih-STRIH-byoot) To share, sell, or otherwise spread something out.

donate (DOH-nayt) To give something in order to help a person or organization.

empower (em-POW-uhr) To give someone a feeling of power.

enact (in-NAKT) To put something into action.

endangered (in-DAYN-jerd) In danger of dying out.

environment (en-VY-ruhn-ment) The conditions that surround a living thing and affect the way it lives.

flexible (FLEK-sih-bul) Being able to move and bend in many ways.

mentor (MEN-tohr) A trusted guide or teacher.

motivate (MOH-tih-vayt) To give someone a reason to do something.

potential (poh-TEN-shuhl) Possible ability; also, existing in a state of possibility.

reciprocal (rih-SIH-pruh-kuhl) Shared, felt, or shown by both sides.

tutor (TOO-tuhr) Someone who teaches one student or a small group of students, or to provide someone with private instruction.

INDEX

PRIMARY SOURCE LIST

Page 4
President John F. Kennedy during his inauguration speech on January 20, 1961, in Washington, D.C. Photograph. George Silk. Now held in the *LIFE* Images Collection by Getty Images.

Page 7
Girl Scouts at White House, Washington, D.C. Photograph. Harris and Ewing. ca. 1916–1919. Now held at the Library of Congress Prints and Photographs Division, Washington, D.C.

Page 15
Navy members serve breakfast to the homeless at Dorothy's Soup Kitchen in Salinas, CA. August 6, 2009. Photograph. Chief Mass Communication Specialist Steve Johnson, U.S. Navy.

WEBSITES

Due to the changing nature of Internet links, PowerKids Press has developed an online list of websites related to the subject of this book. This site is updated regularly. Please use this link to access the list: www.powerkidslinks.com/sociv/csv